A Poetic A-Z of Awesome Animals!

Emilie Lauren Jones

Illustrations and Cover design by Jenna Herman

ISBN : 978-1-9196148-7-8

A Catalogue record for this book is available from the British Library.
Page Layout by Highlight Type Bureau Ltd, Leeds LS20 8LQ
Printed and bound by CPI Group (UK) Ltd, Croydon, CR0 4YY

The paper and board used in this book are natural recyclable products made from wood grown in sustainable forests. The manufacturing processes conform to the environmental regulations of the country of origin.

FSC www.fsc.org
MIX
Paper | Supporting responsible forestry
FSC® C171272

Caboodle Books Ltd.
Riversdale, 8 Rivock Avenue,
Steeton, BD20 6SA, UK.

For Cleo

Contents (by animal)

African Wild Dog

Habitat fragmented

pack members

missing

after two-legged tree cutters

invaded

with their hungry weapons.

Hopefully,

it's not too late

to paint your speckled bodies back

among the broken bracken.

We could learn a lot from you

whose community always offers the first feast

to the young, the weak.

FASCINATING FACT: The African wild dog is also known as the 'painted dog' because of its mottled coat that reminds people of paint splotches.

The Beauty of Blobfish

Silently, steadily, I like to roam
in the depths of the ocean, I feel at home.
My fleshy and droopy, gelatinous form
glides past the coral, peaceful and calm.

With currant eyes, and mouth wide as a creek,
my shape is not odd, just gloriously unique!
I thrive in the deep where the pressure is high,
the water is dark and few dare to pry.

I may not be glamourous or filled with grace
but I'm safe and content in this special place.
I've a heart that is gentle and swelling with love
and a spirit that's free and light as a dove.

FASCINATING FACT: Blobfish don't have bones, muscles or teeth. They were voted the worlds ugliest animal and are the official mascot for the Ugly Animal Preservation Society.

Capybara, Capybara

Capybara, Capybara
giant guinea pig!
Capybara, Capybara
with claws that like to dig.

Capybara, Capybara
makes shallow holes to hide in
Capybara, Capybara
the grasslands are your garden.

Capybara, Capybara
with rough bristles on your back
Capybara, Capybara
and mud between the gaps.

Capybara, Capybara
loves to play with friends
Capybara, Capybara
by the river where you cleanse.

Capybara, Capybara
rolling, climbing, nose rubs
Capybara, Capybara
aunties, uncles, parents, cubs...

Capybara, Capybara
with a friendly, furry tribe
Capybara, Capybara
sips from the water pipe.

Capybara, Capybara
leaps on mother's back
Capybara, Capybara
clings on like a backpack.

Capybara, Capybara
padding through the forest
Capybara, Capybara
and munching on the foliage.

Capybara, Capybara
antenna ears twitching
Capybara, Capybara
predator approaching!

Capybara, Capybara
dashing to the lake
Capybara, Capybara
quickly, hold your breath!

Capybara, Capybara
quiet as rustling reeds
Capybara, Capybara
until the predator leaves.

Capybara, Capybara
relieved that you have won
Capybara, Capybara
paddles off to have more fun.

FASCINATING FACT: The capybara is native to South America and is the largest rodent in the world. They are often thought to be one of the friendliest wild animals.

Donkey – a kenning poem

Tough toothed
fluffy fringed
hay muncher
crunching on sunshine strands.
Carrot wisher
lip curler
begging for treats.
Curious explorer
dust roller
tickling the sky with hooves.
Children carrier
tail swisher
fuss seeker
hoping for human hands to rub behind ears
loyal roamer
trotting, galloping,
fence scratcher
neck nibbler
nudging nosed
social seeker
strong and gentle creature
playful brayer
friends forever.

FASCINATING FACT: Donkeys have best friends! They are very sociable creatures and form deep friendships that last a lifetime.

Epaulette Shark Visits the Beach

The epaulette shark soars through water,
cuts through waves like a knife slicing butter,
smooth and sleek and sports car silver
with fancy black spots for decoration.

But epaulette shark has a strange dream,
something that no one else will believe,
epaulette shark wants to walk under the sea!
'Sharks can't walk!'
the other fish laugh.
'You've got fins not feet,
you're meant to swish and splash.'

But epaulette shark ignored what they said,
she imagined strong fins pushing on sea beds
at first she wobbled and rolled about
but her steps grew firmer and she refused to back out.
She tip-toed, then padded through the Great Barrier
Reef,
then she wandered to shore along the shallow sea.

She played with the coral and brushed past the shells,
and paddled through waves as they swished and they
swelled.
She nibbled on worms then strode to the beach
where humans were chatting and bathing their feet.

One of them spotted her reaching the shore,
they could hardly believe what their eyes saw:
'a walking shark!'
they squealed with delight
and rushed over to see this amazing sight.

She wanted to meet her adoring fans,
so she left the water and wandered onto the sand
she was patted and fussed and photographed,
it filled her with joy to hear people laugh
and not because they found her strange
but because they were all so impressed and amazed
that a shark had a dream and made it come true
and had walked to the beach from out of the blue.

FASCINATING FACT: The Epaulette Shark is often called 'The Walking Shark' due to its ability to walk on its fins. They can walk on the seabed, climb on rocks and have been known to walk on land.

Twelve Foxes - a ghazal

Camouflaged with white and grey. Bushy tailed,
quick-witted, fox thrives.
Warm coat protects against snowflake's ballet.
Bushy tailed, quick-witted, fox thrives.

Large ears dissipate desert heat, with quick paws and
strong leaps,
sensing movement beneath, tasty prey!
Bushy tailed, quick-witted, fox thrives.

Sandy and secretive, snuggling in shared burrows,
dusk arrives, berry picking underway.
Bushy tailed, quick-witted, fox thrives.

Sure-footed mountain climber, curved claws clasp rocky
edges, then cross the sandy plain.
Bushy tailed, quick-witted, fox thrives.

Inky eyed, black-tipped tail as if dipped in paint,
early riser, smile wide as a sunray.
Bushy tailed, quick-witted, fox thrives.

Den-digger, seeking solace during harsh weather,
slow stepper but keen to play.
Bushy tailed, quick-witted, fox thrives.

Making homes by boulders and beaches
Loyal mates, make rodents run away.
Bushy tailed, quick-witted, fox thrives.

Once, almost-extinct then swift recovery occurred
when enemies turned to helpers.
Sun lover bathes on summer days.
Bushy tailed, quick-witted, fox thrives.

Pups pant and play, parents search for water.
This land is shrinking but you continue to find a way.
Bushy tailed, quick-witted, fox thrives.

Middle-Eastern master of song – hisses, trills, whistles
and barks,
Loyal lover with busy nights and restful days.
Bushy tailed, quick-witted, fox thrives.

There's safety among thorn and scrubs, sharp lipped
but trusting.
Himalayan hunter with skills to display.
Bushy tailed, quick-witted, fox thrives.

Trotting past cars passing through your urban
playground,
Shoulders shrug, hips sway.
Bushy tailed, quick-witted, fox thrives.

FASCINATING FACT: There are twelve species of 'true fox' and all of them are mentioned in this poem. In order of appearance they are: Arctic Fox, Fennec Fox, Pale Fox, Blanford's Fox, Cape Fox, Corsac Fox, Tibetan Sand Fox, Swift Fox, Kit Fox, Rüppell's Fox, Bengal Fox and Red Fox.

The Ballad of the Guitar-Playing Grey Squirrel

Nimble grey squirrel
was looking for fun
but the swings in the playground
were silent and still
so she darted and dashed
through the trees
in the park,
crossed the road,
crossed the field
and found a small home.

She clambered up tiles
on a rickety roof
then crawled through a hole
into a warm room.
'An attic!' she whispered
then began to explore
as moonlight flew through
a gap up above.

She scurried and scrambled
over pictures and toys
until something she stepped on
made a brilliant noise!
A dusty guitar lay on the floor
squirrel decided to twang it,
just once more...

At first with her teeth then again with her claws,
squirrel played several notes
then brought in some chords
till the attic was filled with a majestic din
and when she finished one song, she started again.

Below, in his bed, a little boy woke,
he shuffled and sighed
then sat up, confused.
What was that noise coming down from the ceiling?
He couldn't quite grasp what he was hearing.
It sounded just like his mum's old guitar
but who would be strumming at this early hour?
He snuck out of bed and climbed up the steps,
pushed up the hatch and peeked through the gap.

His eyes adjusted to the dark of the attic
and scanned the room for the source of the racket.
He blinked a few times to be sure it was real,
that there, in his house, was a guitar playing squirrel.
If squirrel had seen him, she might have been startled
but her eyes were closed and her head was bobbing
so he stared and smiled with his fingers tap-tapping.

When the tune finished, he couldn't help but applaud
and grey squirrel jumped, shocked she'd been caught.
With a flick of her tail, she darted away,
dashing over old dolls and dusty pictures in frames.
The boy tried to call her but he was too late,
the guitar playing squirrel had run far away.
The next night, the boy made a snack before bed,
a plate stacked with raisins and peanut butter spread.
He said goodnight to his mum and when she closed the door,
he waited a while before his mission began.
Sneaking up to the attic as quiet as a whisper,
he left the plate of goodies especially for squirrel,
he carefully placed it next to her guitar
then made his descent back to his room.

A few hours later, he was jolted awake
by the twang of guitar strings and chink of a plate.
He lay and he listened, with a grin on his face,
as the notes danced together and the rhythm increased.
He stayed snuggled up, under his duvet
while above him, squirrel continued to play.

Now every night squirrel munches on her
peanut butter gift
and in return she plays the boy all her favourite hits.
She finds it far more fun than roaming the cold night
streets
and the boy basks in guitar lullabies before he falls
asleep.

FASCINATING FACT: Grey squirrels are very athletic! Their sharp claws and strong hind legs enable them to climb vertical surfaces like trees, walls and bird feeders.

Mysterious Thief or The Herring Gull

A croissant on the breakfast table disappeared from
its plate
with just a few crumbs left behind, the culprit
couldn't wait
to feast on crispy, buttered pastry
filled with tasty cactus jam.

When Olivia went swimming at the sandy beach
she took off both her flip flops before entering the sea
but when returning from her dip
only one was left so now she flips instead of flops.

Abdullah was a fan of tomato sauce and chips
but when he closed his eyes to put one to his lips,
he found it snatched out of his hand
and couldn't understand where it had gone.

Sara's supermarket shelf was stacked with lots of packets,
then suddenly from three aisles down she was alerted to
a racket,
three shiny silver packages had been taken off display
the culprit didn't pay but left a grey feather in their
place.
Another time in Jersey, George was licking chocolate
ice cream

he thought he heard a giant beak release a thrilled scream,
but all he really knows is that his cone then disappeared
it's very clear the thief is clever and likes a sugary treat.

Aisha was very careful when she put the rubbish out
the bag, well-tied and neatly placed without a doubt
but later on, the sack was shredded and there was litter on the ground
all around were claw marks and evidence of pecks.

Although we're lacking evidence, I think we have a suspect:
the criminal we're looking for was rapid as he swept
with wings, a beak and claws, he had motive and intent
and on his escape, often left a feather.

FASCINATING FACT: Gulls have large brains that make them able to adapt quickly to the challenges and fast changing environment of urban areas. Known for nicking ice creams and other tasty treats, according to one survey, Herring Gulls were successful in 50% of their stealing attempts!

Impala Wins Olympic Gold

The Animal Olympics were on their final day –
elephant smashed the weightlifting,
Cheetah won the sprint,
and it turned out chimp was very good
when it came to BMX.

Next up was the long jump –
the crowd had gathered round.
Tree Frog was the favourite
and he did very well,
Dolphin was disqualified
for getting everybody soaked
and Flea was super launching
over 200 times his length
(although, giraffe beat his record
by taking just one step).

Then came gentle Impala,
who quietly trotted up.
'Oh, surely she can't leap that well?'
Someone behind her scoffed.
'Her tail is soft, her legs are thin
and those horns are far too high.'
Impala simply looked away
she knew that she would try.

She had a decent run up,
the wind flew past her ears
and when she reached the perfect point,
her back legs turned to springs.
Impala flew above their heads,
her tail fluffed like a cloud.
And when she finally landed
there were cheers from all the crowd.

And that is how Impala won
the Animal Olympics,
now she proudly prances through the woods,
her golden medal swinging.

FASCINATING FACT: Impalas are medium-sized antelopes that are excellent jumpers. They can reach heights of over 10 feet (3m) and jump a distance of over 33 feet (10m.)

Japanese Crane - a tanka

One-thousand-year friend,
ruby crowned raucous dancer
wide winged squawking flight,
you soar over swamp and sea
granting wishes, bringing peace.

FASCINATING FACT: Japanese cranes are extremely rare and are only usually found in Hokkaido, the northernmost island of Japan. They are considered a national treasure and symbols of longevity, good luck and loyalty.

Koala

Cute koala cuddles her eucalyptus kingdom,
curved claws clasp a branch,
face cupped between leaves.
Keen thumbs collect treasure –
Koala crunches,
consuming cooling citrus.
Wisps of coal-coloured fur
cover her cheeks.
Closing her eyes,
she recharges –
clever koala
conserving precious energy.

Australia's celebrated creature,
she curls up in the cold
then unfolds across tree limbs
under a cosy sun.

FACINATING FACT: A koala's diet consists almost entirely of eucalyptus leaves. They spend a lot of time resting and can sleep up to 20 hours a day!

A Leech's Love Song

Wading feet feel for the floor,
Leech watches,
overwhelmed at the beauty
of shimmering skin,
delicate as marsh marigolds.
Leech slithers,
slides over the curve of ankle
then hugs the little toe,
kisses it with his snout
and drinks.

FASCINATING FACT: Leeches have been used by doctors for a very long time. When certain leeches bite a person, they release a special liquid into their skin which helps keep their blood flowing smoothly.

Mosquito

I grew from the energy my mother managed to acquire
from the unduveted arms of sleeping humans
or from late night feasting on sockless ankles.

I grew from an egg that floated alongside a hundred siblings
from the sticky raft that held us together
and summer's stench of stagnant water.

I grew from stretching and wiggling,
from a two-week snorkel trip through a murky pool
and filtering through algae for food.

I grew from shaking off my skin several times
from shedding old habits, embracing transformation,
a willingness to reform, renew, renovate.

I grew from floating, tumbling across the liquid surface
from letting the breeze send me where it pleased
and building the casing of my new home.

I grew from sealing myself away and hoping for the best,
from the hardening of my hidden body
and the joy of breaking free.

I grew from power of the full moon
from sniffing out the heat of human breath
and following the sweet scent of carbon dioxide.

I grew from sneaking through open windows,
from looking for limbs that offer energy
and feasting, feasting...

I grew from gaining enough energy to make hundreds
of eggs
from carefully laying long lines of them
and watching them stick together and float away.

FASCINATING FACT: While all mosquitoes feed on nectar and plant sap, only the female mosquitoes bite. This is because they need the protein from blood to produce their eggs.

Narwhal

dives into ocean's embrace,
glides through dancing undercurrents
then emerges
ribboned tusk first
ripping through the icy surface –
a real-life sea unicorn
whose celestial skin shimmers silver-blue.
His curious clicks and whistles
echo through this ice kingdom,
the giant tusk, his crown –
a warrior king fighting dancing waves
beneath the shards of ice.

FASCINATING FACT: Only the male narwhals have a tusk (which is actually an enlarged tooth). The tusk can grow up to 3 metres (10ft) long.

Conversations with an Orangutan

We meet as agreed, beneath this tree.
Not sure whether to hug or shake hands
we stand, awkwardly at first,
until she motions and we sit down.
Her curved shoulders
remind me how mum says not to slump,
she shrugs as if sensing what I'm thinking.
I tell her I envy her natural ginger hair,
mine comes from a bottle.
'Plastic?' she asks,
I nod

then enquire about where she grew up,
was she always from round here?
'No,' she says
the monsters took her home away
with loud machines and metal blades
and now the trees she swung on in childhood are gone.
But what about her friends?
'Scattered,' she says
like berries dropped from the beaks of birds.
I hold my hand up as if touching a mirror
she responds
her palm slightly larger,
fingernails wider, creased.
Is she safe?
'For now,' she says,
birdsong masks the distant sound
of falling branches.

FASCINATING FACT: humans and orangutans share approximately 97% of their DNA. All three orangutan species are critically endangered. Their main threat is loss of habitat, caused by logging, forest fires and making way for oil palm plantations.

Python – a perfectly pleasing poem

Peaceful python pours itself into a pot
Professional python participates in project planning
Poorly, pale python practises patience and positivity
Painter python picks pastels from its palette –
preferring pretty pinks and purples
Pretend python performs in pantomimes with pizzazz
Pilgrim python prepares, practising peculiar phrases
Photographer python preens, poses
Preservationist python praises photosynthesis –
planting poppies and pines
Professor python plots pie-charts
Plural pythons play and prattle
Pouncing python picks its prey
Pleased python pauses upon a pile of puffy pillows
Popular python, pandered, proud
Portrait python – picture-perfect put up in a porch
Philosophical python ponders
Penultimate python prefers this position
Published python pens playful poems.

FASCINATING FACT: Pythons are nonvenomous snakes. There are about 40 recognised species of pythons, making them one of the largest families of snakes in the whole world.

A Quokka's Recipe for Happiness

Ingredients

- A litre of friendship
- 5 teaspoons of curiosity
- 2 large helpings of caressing claws
- 1 portion of moonlight
- 4 sprigs of prickly plants
- 300ml of confidence
- A munching of purple flowers
- A sprinkle of smiles

Method

1. Mix the prickly plants with the litre of friendship, enjoy company and cosying up next to spiky leaves while you sleep
2. Stir to create a safe space filled with love
3. Slice the curiosity and spread excitedly
4. Hold the moonlight over the bowl and watch as the mixture becomes more vibrant
5. Meanwhile, add the touch of claws carefully caressing fur, there's nothing better than a good pampering
6. Next, pour in the 300ml of confidence, appreciate your cuteness and pose for plenty of selfies (in exchange for cuddles, of course)

7. Add the munching of purple flowers as decoration but don't expect them to remain uneaten for long, sweet treats enable energy
8. Serve warm and bubbling with a big grin

FASCINATING FACT: Resembling a kangaroo in shape but about the size of a cat, the quokka possesses a charming teddy bear-like face. Renowned as "the happiest animal in the world," it maintains a perpetual smile and exhibits a friendly nature.

Rabbit – concrete poem

Poem text:

Lepus leaps, lucky feet land. My silent friend speaks in head nudges. He hops happily hoping for a cabbage leaf or ear massage. Tame hearted but wild pawed.

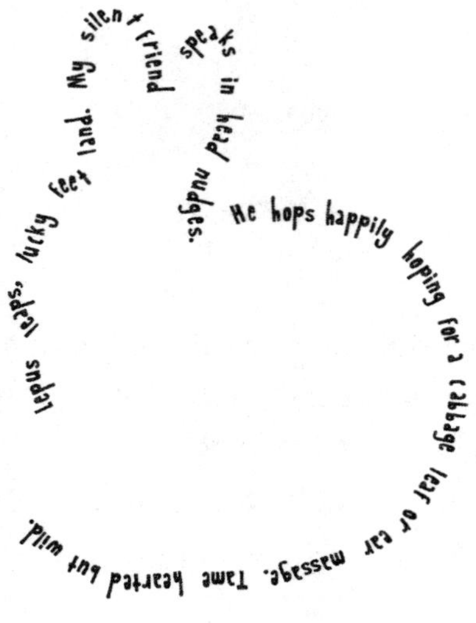

FASCINATING FACT: The Latin word for rabbit is ‘lepus’, this word is also used to refer to hares. Rabbits communicate with each other using body language including: flopping, doing ‘binkies’ (a kind of excited hop) and loafing when they are happy, or thumping and nipping when they are upset or scared.

Parastratiosphecomyia Sphecomyioides or Soldier Fly?

Perhaps it's silly to have a name so long
After all, isn't 'Soldier Fly' just fine?
Replicating its waspish hero,
Armoured with stripes,
Seeking sugarcane roots to slurp on –
The tastiest treat imaginable!
Reacting fast to swatting hands
And buzzing back to swampy lands
The soldier fly (we'll call it that)
Inclined to recline in the sun
On its leafy hammock
Serene, wings folded behind its head,
Patiently waiting for wispy clouds to pass,
Holding on to happiness.
Each day takes a similar form:
Chomp, chill and remain cautious of predators
Only pausing this routine to create
More maggots
Yellowy-brown and transforming
Into wiggling larva, licking algae
Admiring the sliminess of your new home.

Soldier Fly (does it mind if we call it that?)
Perhaps it likes the grander title
Happy that reflects its metallic strength

Emphasises its abilities to scavenge, to survive
Captures the grand lines on veiny wings?
Occupying gaps beneath lumps of soil
Moving over wetlands
Yearning for the stink of stagnant water.
It seeks sugary nectar
Often finding joy inside flower petals,
Idolising the sun filled sky
Dipping six legs into marshland.
Exceptionally unique insect named...
Soldier Fly (or does it prefer Parastratiosphecomyia
Sphecomyioides?)

FASCINATING FACT: A species of soldier fly, Parastratiosphecomyia sphecomyioides, is the longest scientific name for an animal.

Tiger – a golden shovel poem

"The eyes of the tiger are the brightest of any animal on Earth. They blaze back the ambient light with awe-inspiring intensity." - Billy Arjan Singh, conservationist and tiger lover

Your fir is fire, coal and smoke, and **the**
flames that spark from your **eyes**
illuminate reflections **of**
sprawling petals and fern-lined forest floor. You follow **the**
advice of the strangler fig whose roots creep like **tiger**
paws, it's possible to survive this harsh paradise when you **are**
fierce flame rising from the ash of your underbelly. Even **the**
very **brightest**
midnight stars are convinced your eyes are made **of**
swirling amber and **any**
more-timid **animal**
dashes away from the quiet thud of heavy paw pressing **on**
moist **earth.**
You parade past rushing waterfalls, knowing **they**
could never dampen your majestic **blaze.**
In your game, fire beats water. Leaves step **back**
to allow you to pass. **The**
spiked fur of your tongue laps the riverbank while **ambient**
sounds swirl above: birdsong blooms from branches and **light**
reaches through cracks in the canopy, meeting **with**
water droplets that rest on your back, an **awe-inspiring**
orange, and your eyes lit with a burning **intensity.**

FASCINATING FACT: The largest member of the cat family, each tiger has a unique pattern on their coat. They are incredibly strong and agile but also highly endangered.

Umbrella Bird - a limerick

There once was a bird with a hood
who realised his life was quite good
because when it rained
his body contained
a perfect defence to the flood.

FASCINATING FACT: Umbrella birds can be found in the rainforest and are named after the crest on the top of their head. It is fairly slow and clunky and can only fly short distances.

Superhero Snail

Volcano snail doesn't have a cape
or star in a blockbuster movie series
but he's a marvel of the natural world:
iron shelled; bullet cased,
no need for food – he can recharge
like a character from a PlayStation.
His feet are formed from shards of metal
and he lives in the furnace
of an underwater volcano.

FASCINATING FACT: The volcano snail is the only animal on earth whose body is made up of iron. They can even be picked up by a magnet!

Wolf - concrete poem

Poem Text:
Born unseeing into a silent world but strengthened by mother's milk, you grow into a wild wanderer with superpowered senses – a stick snaps six miles away, your ears rotate, confirm it's safe. Rolling and running with pack pals until incisors seek sustenance. Padded paws prowl, hoping for hoofed footprints to hunt down. When full, you climb to high ground and howl gratitude to the waxing moon.

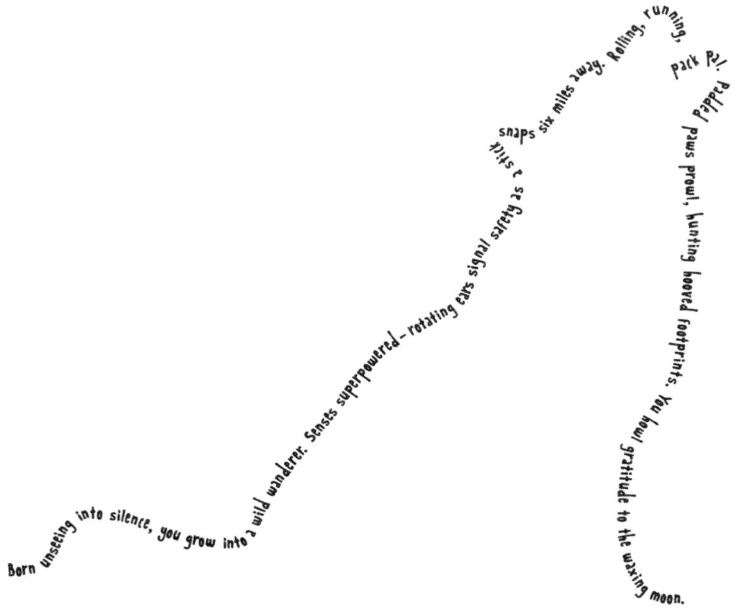

Born unseeing into silence, you grow into a wild wanderer. Senses superpowered – rotating ears signal safety as a stick snaps six miles away. Rolling, running, pack pal. Padded paws prowl, hunting hooved footprints. You howl gratitude to the waxing moon.

FASCINATING FACT: Wolf pups are born deaf and blind with bright blue eyes, but within a month of being born they are able to see and hear. This is when they start to explore and play. Adult wolves can hear sounds that are up to 9.7km (six miles) away in the forest.

X-ray Fish

Snap a glimpse
of transparent fins,
skeleton swish
flashing past the riverbank.
Blood beats below the surface
of skin so thin it lets the light in,
so strong it holds an entire system –
a machine of bone and vessels.
Dorsal fin flies above –
a flag of white, black, yellow
celebrating the fortress of your body.

FASCINATING FACT: Known for their peaceful nature, x-ray fish have a transparent body so you can see their skeleton and internal organs through their skin.

Yeti Crab

'Come here!' calls the Yeti Crab
'I'll show you around my world...
Once you've seen it, you'll agree
it's the greatest place you've ever been.'

'First, you might like to meet
some of my amazing mates,
I only have five thousand
so I'm sure you'll learn their names...'

Yeti crab crawls over
heaps of his fidgety friends,
rolling around like popcorn kernels
on the rocky seabed.

'Next, we'll dine in luxury
at the finest restaurant,
I worked all week to grow these treats
on my hairy arms!'

Once crab has finished munching food
from between his brush-like bristles
he clicks a claw and guides us
to his favourite feature.

'Here is the greatest luxury
that lays here in the dark,
the one that gathers crowds of crabs –
the tremendous thermal spa!'

And so, we laze away the day
resting by the whooshing vents –
it really is quite special,
this jacuzzi just for crabs.

FASCINATING FACT: The yeti crab gets its name from its hairy 'arms'. Their main diet is bacteria which they capture thanks to these bristly hairs.

Blueprints

Warm wind rustles through the grassland,
where the young zebras play on the plain.
Black and white bar charts across their backs,
their tails flick away flies,
hooves skip across the dry ground
then rear up, nose to nose, to see who's tallest.
Mother zebra watches
little legs trot towards her
her eyes scanning the barcode of his skin –
the best pattern in the world.

FASCINATING FACT: A zebras stripes are totally unique. The pattern and arrangement of their stripes are like a fingerprint, meaning no two zebras have exactly the same stripe pattern.

An ABC of Caring for the Planet

A was in awe of the natural world
B basked in the beauty of buttercups and blue whales
C cared for all creatures, even the crawly and slimy ones
D didn't mean to cause destruction
E encouraged everyone to examine bad habits but
F fostered a passion for fast fashion and
G got used to going in the car instead of walking
H hoped that the others would hear her concerns but
I remained indifferent
J joked that just one person couldn't make a difference
K kept meaning to...
L loved all living things but also liked leaving all the lights on
M muttered and moaned, made more promises and
N never noticed what needed recycling but
O began to realise there was only one planet
P planted trees and plenty of flowers
Q quietly quashed her plastic bag habit
R reduced her waste by reusing and recycling
S started supporting sustainable companies
T tried his best
U understood more could be done
V veered away from sprays with chemicals
W wanted to wade in sewage free waves

X examined his carbon footprint, crossed off a list of excuses
Y yearned for fresh air and freedom
Z said zero-emissions isn't a dream,
Z said we need to wake up.

FASCINATING FACT: The well-being of animals is intertwined with our own well-being and the health of our planet. Healthy and thriving animal populations contribute to a balanced and resilient environment, which ultimately benefits human societies as well.

Alphabet Kids

I don't fit in,
I'm not one of those alphabet kids
who knows their place in line,
I find myself in the wrong space at the wrong time.
I daydream when I should be writing,
mind drifting from maths
to the crow outside the window,
to that day two years ago…
I'm not one of those alphabet kids
who get ten on the spelling tests
and have a licence to write with a pen.
I paint accidental artworks on my shirt
with food dropped from a spoon
and after PE class,
I often model my clothes inside out.
I'm not one of those alphabet kids,
who can throw and catch and run really quick
but I always turn up, excited to learn
even when I leave my pencil case at home.

I'm not one of those alphabet kids,

I don't fit in,

there are too many letters that can describe me:

like 'H' for human and 'K' for kid

or 'I' for being super imaginative,

'F' for funny (I'm hilarious!),

'C' for caring, 'A' for ambitious,

'P' for polite and 'L' for loving,

I suppose I should mention 'U' for unique,

because there's lots of letters to describe me.

I don't really fit into a neatly formed line

but with all these letters and adjectives,

I guess you could say I'm an alphabet kid!

That's One Cool Cat!

Follow these instructions to make an awesome origami cat:

What you need: A4 paper (any colour!), a felt tip pen and scissors

1. Take an A4 piece of paper

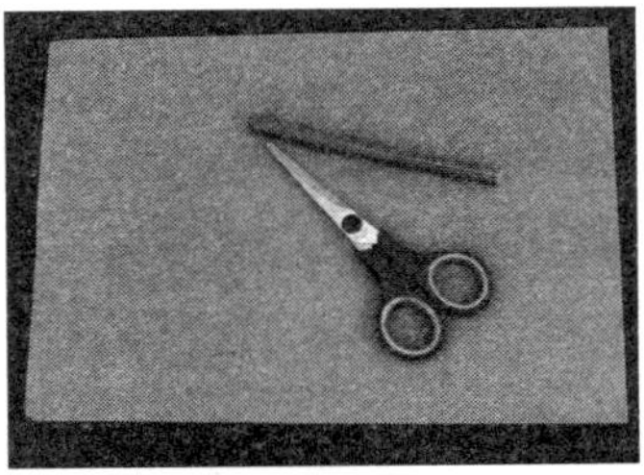

2. Make it into a square by folding the top left corner down until it reaches the bottom of the paper.

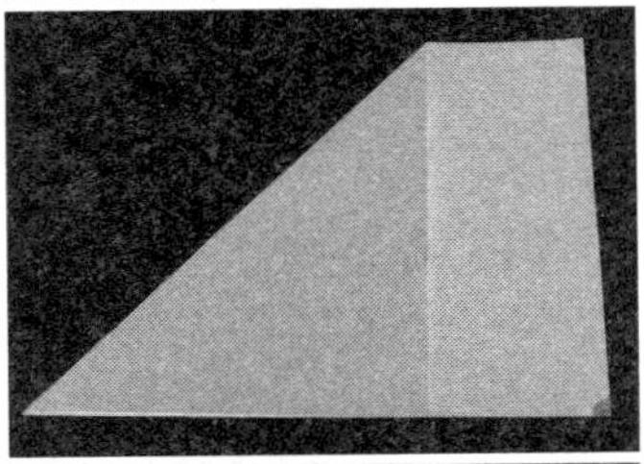

3. Make a crease mark and cut along the fold to leave a square piece of paper.

4. Unfold the paper. You have a square! Now we can start making our cat...

5. Take the bottom corner and fold it diagonally to meet the top corner, creating a triangle.

6. Now, fold this triangle in half again by bringing the top corner to meet the bottom corner.

7. Carefully unfold the paper back to the triangle shape in the previous step.

8. Turn the paper so the point of the triangle is facing upwards.

9. Create the ears by folding the left and right corners of the triangle up at an angle, forming two triangular flaps on top.

10. Fold a small portion of the top point down, creating a slight crease.

11. Flip the paper over to the other side.

12. Let your creativity shine! Using the felt tip pen, draw eyes and whiskers on the figure to give it a playful appearance.

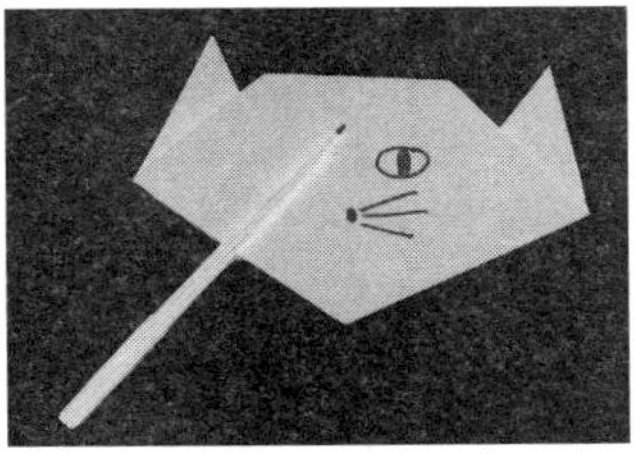

13. Enjoy your origami creation! You could even use it as a bookmark.

How to be a Planet-Saving Superhero!

Being eco-friendly means doing things that are kind to the Earth and all the animals that live here. It's like being a superhero for the planet and the animals!

Reduce, Reuse, Recycle: Use reusable items like water bottles, lunch boxes, and shopping bags. Remember to recycle paper, plastic, and glass by putting them in the right bins. Animals need clean air, water, and soil, just like we do. When we throw away lots of rubbish or pollution, it can make them sick. But when we're eco-friendly and keep the Earth clean, animals can stay healthy and happy too.

Save Energy: Be an energy superhero! Turn off lights, TV, and video games when you're not using them. Remind your family to close doors and windows to keep the house cozy without wasting energy. Some animals are in danger of disappearing forever because things are changing too fast. Being eco-friendly helps slow down those changes and gives endangered animals a better chance to survive and live with us.

Water Conservation: Save water like a pro! Turn off the tap while brushing your teeth, and let grown-ups know if there's a leak. Use water wisely during playtime too! Clean water is super important for animals that live in the rivers, lakes, and oceans. When we use water wisely and don't waste it, we help keep animals' homes healthy too.

Plant Trees: Help the Earth breathe by planting trees! Join tree-planting events or grow your own tree or shrub in your garden. Trees make our air cleaner and cooler, provide oxygen and offer places for animals to live and nest.

Use Eco-friendly Transportation: Try green ways to move around. Walk, bike, or use the bus with your family instead of always using the car. It's fun and good for the planet!

Compost: Turn food scraps and garden waste into plant food! Learn how to compost, and if you have a garden, ask your parents/guardians if you can start a compost bin.

Support Wildlife: Become a friend of nature! Set up a bird feeder or plant flowers that butterflies love. Create safe spots for animals in your garden or local park.

Educate Others: Be an eco-teacher! Share what you've learned about taking care of the Earth with your friends, family, and classmates. Together, we can make a big difference!

Reduce Plastic Use: Fight plastic pollution! Use a reusable water bottle instead of single-use ones. Use a metal straw and avoid plastic bags to protect our ocean friends. Animals can get caught in things like plastic bags or nets. It can hurt them a lot! When we use less plastic and recycle more, we make sure animals don't get trapped in things they shouldn't.

Join Environmental Clubs: Be a planet protector with friends! Join an environmental club or youth group. You'll get to do cool things like cleanups and learn more about helping the planet. Being eco-friendly means we care about every animal, big or small. From tiny insects to giant elephants, they all matter, and we want to make sure they're safe and happy.

Remember, every small action counts, and you can be a superhero for the Earth every day! By being eco-friendly, we show love and respect for all the animals on our amazing planet. Together, we can make a big difference and create a world where animals can live happily and safely alongside us!

Write Your Own Poems with these Poetry Challenges

These writing challenges are inspired by some of the poems in this book. Now you can have a go at creating your own animal poems too:

Challenge 1

Take a look at *Capybara, Capybara'* on page X

This poem uses repetition to create a strong rhythm. Use repetition to create a poem about an animal of your choice, it doesn't have to rhyme but it can do. Remember to use lots of adjectives.

Challenge 2

Read *Donkey – a kenning poem* on page X

Kennings are a very old form of poetry, and have been found in examples of Anglo-Saxon and Old Norse writings, but they are still great fun to write today.

A kenning is a unique way to describe someone or something. Often, they are made up of two nouns or a noun and a verb. For example, the donkey is described as a 'hay muncher' because he loves eating hay and a 'fuss seeker' because he enjoys attention from humans, especially having his ears tickled!

Can you write your own kenning poem to describe yourself, a friend or family member?

Challenge 3

In *Conversations with an Orangutan* on page X, the narrator talks to an orangutan and discovers why the species is endangered. If you could talk to any animal, what would you ask? What would their response be? Perhaps your conversation could be with a pet, it could be with an insect at the park or an animal you've never seen. Turn this conversation into a poem and add in some amazing adjectives to describe your chosen creature.

Challenge 4

Parastratiosphecomyia Sphecomyioides or Soldier Fly? on page X is an acrostic poem. This means that the title or subject of the poem is written vertically down the left-hand side of the page and they become the first letter of every line. The Latin name for the soldier fly, which is used in this poem, is a very long title! Something simpler could be 'dog'. Simple acrostics can even have just one word per line. Here's an example of a short acrostic about a dog (see how the first letter of every line makes the word 'dog'):

Delightful, playful
Old friend
Golden fur and wagging tail

Challenge 5

Take a look at the two concrete poems, *Rabbit* on page X and *Wolf* on page X.

Trace or draw a picture of your favourite animal on a plain piece of paper. On scrap paper or in your notebook, draft a short poem about that animal. Think about what it's doing, how it moves and what noises it makes. Write your poem around the edge of your drawing to create a concrete poem. If you have too many words you can go around your picture twice or use the extra words to create grass, flowers or water. If you need a few extra words then think about some strong adjectives or verbs that you can add in.

Trickier Challenges

Tricky Challenge One

Have a go at your own ghazal. You can use *Twelve Foxes – a ghazal* on page X to help with the structure.

A ghazal (pronounced guzzle) originated in Arabia in the 7th century. The poem traditionally has at least five stanzas.

The first stanza sets up the rhyme scheme and refrain (the underlined words are the rhyme scheme and the bold text is the refrain):

Camouflaged with white and grey. ***Bushy tailed, quick-witted, fox thrives.***

Warm coat protects against snowflake's ballet. ***Bushy tailed, quick-witted, fox thrives.***

All the following stanzas follow the same pattern as each other, the refrain appears at the end of each stanza and the word before the refrain follows the rhyme scheme established in the first stanza:

Large ears dissipate dessert heat, with quick paws and strong leaps,

sensing movement beneath, tasty prey! ***Bushy tailed, quick-witted, fox thrives.***

Every stanza is written as a couplet (two lines).

Tricky Challenge Two

Take a look at *Japanese Crane – a tanka* on page X

Tanka poems originate from Japan and are another ancient poetic form, the earliest examples we know of are from at least the 9th century. Tanka are always about nature and/or feelings and use strong imagery to describe the setting.

The first three lines of the tanka are actually a haiku (another form of ancient Japanese poem). They don't rhyme. The first line has 5 syllables, the second line has 7 syllables and the third line has 5 syllables.

To make it into a tanka, you need to add another two lines, each of these additional lines have seven syllables and they don't need to rhyme.

So, the poem should have a total of five lines and follow the following syllable format: 5,7,5,7,7

The easiest way to count syllables is to tap or clap them out.

Tricky Challenge Three

Python – a perfectly pleasing poem on page X, is a type of poem called a tautogram. This means that every word (or nearly every word) in the poem starts with the same first letter.

Choose a letter of the alphabet and spend five minutes creating a 'word bank' by writing down as many words as you can that begin with that letter. It might be a good idea to use a dictionary to help you.

See which of these words work well together to tell a story and then use these to start your poem. Tautograms can often be nonsense poems so have fun playing with the words and seeing what you create.

A Glossary of Poetic Terms

Acrostic – a poem in which the first letter of each line, when read vertically from top to bottom, forms a word, phrase, or name.
Alliteration – the repetition of consonant sounds in nearby words, for example 'broken bracken'
Alphabet poem – also called an 'ABC poem', every line of the poem begins with the next letter of the alphabet.
Anaphora – a poem that uses the repetition of a word or phrase at the beginning of lines.
Assonance – like alliteration, this is the repetition of a certain vowel sound in nearby words
Concrete poem – also known as a 'shape poem', the poem is written in the shape of the poem's topic
Free Verse – any form of poetry that does not rely on consistent patterns of rhyme or metre.
Ghazal – an ancient poetic form originating in Arabic. A ghazal is constructed with couplets, repeated words, and rhyming words.
Golden Shovel – a modern poetic form where the poet takes an existing poem or quote and uses each word as the end word of each line in their poem.
Kenning poem – a type of poetic form that originated in Old Norse and Old English. It uses metaphorical phrases or compound words to describe a person, place, or thing. For example, a donkey can be described as a 'hay muncher'.

Limerick – A short, humorous verse that is usually nonsensical. It has five lines that rhyme using an 'aabba' pattern.

Metaphor – a word or phrase literally denoting one kind of object or idea is used in place of another to suggest a likeness or analogy between them. For example, saying a tiger's fur is fire.

Metre – a regular rhythm or structure.

Onomatopoeia – a word that sounds like what it means. For example, click or snap.

Personification – giving human characteristics to nonhuman things like animals or inanimate objects.

Repetition – saying or writing a word or phrase over and over again.

Rhyme – where two words have the same, or similar, sounds at the end.

Rhythm – the beat or the flow of a poem.

Stanza – a stanza is a group of lines within a poem, usually set apart by a blank line or indentation. Songs have verses and poems have stanzas.

Simile – like a metaphor but using the word 'like' or 'as' to show there is a likeness. For example, 'Capybara clings on like a backpack.'

Syllable – a part of a word that contains a single sound, you can clap out the parts of a word to find the syllables. For example, 'tiger' has two syllables (ti – ger) but 'wolf' just has one.

Tanka – an ancient Japanese form of poetry made up of five lines. The lines have 5,7,5,7,7 syllables.

Tautogram – a poem where all (or nearly all) the words start with the same letter

Test your animal knowledge with these fun quizzes! How many will you get right and what new facts will you learn?!

Quiz 1

1. What is the largest land animal on Earth?
a) Elephant
b) Giraffe
c) Lion
d) Hippopotamus

2. Which of these animals can fly?
a) Penguin
b) Dolphin
c) Bat
d) Emu

3. Which animal is known for its ability to mimic the sounds of its surroundings, including human speech?
a) Parrot
b) Elephant
c) Gorilla
d) Dolphin

4. Which animal lives in the Arctic?
a) Polar bear
b) Penguin
c) Koala
d) Seal

5. Which animal has the longest neck?
a) Elephant
b) Giraffe
c) Gecko
d) Rhinoceros

6. Which animal, that lives in water, breathes through blowholes on top of its head?
a) Octopus
b) Turtle
c) Whale
d) Crab

7. Which of these creatures can climb trees?
a) Squirrel
b) Rabbit
c) Deer
d) Hyena

8. Which animal can survive the longest without water?
a) Camel
b) Hedgehog
c) Dog
d) Cat

9. Which of these clever critters can change its colour to blend in with its surroundings?

a) Lion
b) Cheetah
c) Chameleon
d) Tiger

10. Which mammal is capable of echolocation, using sound waves to navigate and locate objects?

a) Bat
b) Giraffe
c) Guinea Pig
d) Kangaroo

Quiz 1 Answers:

1. Elephant
2. Bat
3. Parrot
4. Polar Bear
5. Giraffe
6. Whale
7. Squirrel
8. Camel
9. Chameleon
10. Bat

Quiz 2

1. Which of the following is a marsupial?
a) Lion
b) Koala
c) Tiger
d) Cheetah

2. Which animal is known for its soft fur, whiskers, and ability to land on its feet?
a) Cat
b) Dog
c) Bird
d) Fish

3. Which mammal has the largest brain?
a) Elephant
b) Dolphin
c) Gorilla
d) Human

4. What is the fastest land animal on the planet?
a) Cheetah
b) Lion
c) Jaguar
d) Tiger

5. Which animal is known for its ability to spray a strong-smelling liquid as a defence mechanism?
a) Skunk
b) Hedgehog
c) Ferret
d) Rabbit

6. Which of these is not a reptile?
a) Turtle
b) Lizard
c) Crocodile
d) Spider

7. All insects have the same number of legs, how many?
a) 4
b) 5
c) 6
d) 7

8. Dolphins, elephants and gorillas all have what?
a) A tail
b) An amazing memory
c) Tusks
d) Claws

9. Which animal has the longest migration route of any mammal on Earth?
a) Zebra
b) Wildebeest
c) Monarch butterfly
d) Arctic tern

10. Which bird has the largest wingspan?
a) Sparrow
b) Albatross
c) Falcon
d) Owl

Quiz 2 Answers:

1. Koala
2. Cat
3. Elephant
4. Cheetah
5. Skunk
6. Spider
7. 6 legs
8. An amazing memory
9. Monarch butterfly
10. Albatross

Quiz 3

1. Which animal is known as the "King of the Jungle"?
a) Lion
b) Tiger
c) Elephant
d) Gorilla

2. Which animal is often associated with Australia and carries its young in a pouch?
a) Kangaroo
b) Koala
c) Platypus
d) Dolphin

3. Why are flamingos pink?
a) They get it from their food
b) They change colour in the sun
c) They are born pink
d) Because they paint themselves pink.

4. Which animal is also called the "unicorn of the sea"?
a) Dolphin
b) Narwhal
c) Penguin
d) Shark

5. Garden snails have more teeth than almost any other animal, how many?

a) 20
b) 200
c) 2,000
d) 20,000

6. Which is the largest species of shark?

a) Great White Shark
b) Hammerhead Shark
c) Tiger Shark
d) Whale Shark

7. Which animal is the symbol of peace?

a) Dove
b) Swan
c) Peacock
d) Parrot

8. Which species includes the smallest mammal in the world?

a) Fox
b) Rat
c) Shrew
d) Squirrel

9. Which of the following best describes the appearance of a blobfish?
a) Spiky and colourful
b) Slender and graceful
c) Squishy and gelatinous
d) Furry and playful

10. Which animal has a reputation for being the slowest-moving mammal?
a) Sloth
b) Cheetah
c) Gazelle
d) Ostrich

Quiz 3 Answers:

1. Lion
2. Kangaroo
3. They get it from their food
4. Narwhal
5. 20,000 teeth
6. Whale Shark
7. Dove
8. Shrew
9. Squishy and gelatinous
10. Sloth

Acknowledgements

There are many people I need to thank. Firstly, Authors Abroad and Caboodle Books, who are amazing to work with and extremely supportive. Thank you especially to Yvonne and Robin, without your encouragement and patience this book wouldn't exist. Thanks also to Jenna Herman for her creative brilliance, and Angela at Highlight for pulling it all together into the finished book format.

There are many other organisations who have had a hugely positive impact on my writing journey, including Writing West Midlands, Nine Arches Press, Coventry Library Services and Positive Images Festival (who gave me my first paid booking and have continued to support my work all these years later!).

As a writer, I have also benefitted from the support of groups including Fire & Dust, Coventry Stanza, Broken Duck Poets and the Coventry Writer's Group. I encourage anyone interested in writing to find their local writing and poetry communities.

I couldn't put a thank you list together without mentioning my amazing parents who have always given me their love and support. Thank you for encouraging me to follow my poetry dream! Plus, an additional thanks to my mum for all our conversations about weird animals of the world!

I am also hugely grateful to all of the schools who invite me to work with their students – I hope you enjoy these poems!

About the author

Emilie Lauren Jones was Coventry's first Poet Laureate. Her words have featured on local and national radio and television. As well as performing, writing commissions and participating in poetry projects, Emilie facilitates workshops for adults and young people, and enjoys visiting schools, care homes, community groups (and anywhere else!) to share her love of words.

An enthusiast of all animals, Emilie has shared her home with rabbits, guinea pigs, fish and hamsters. She also currently lives with her daughter Cleo, and her mum, who helps tidy up after them all!

To enquire about booking Emilie for an event or school visit, please contact the Authors Abroad team at: general@caboodlebooks.co.uk